Christopher Stuart Patterson

The Political Crisis of 1861.

A Reply to Mr. Blaine

Christopher Stuart Patterson

The Political Crisis of 1861.
A Reply to Mr. Blaine

ISBN/EAN: 9783337080716

Printed in Europe, USA, Canada, Australia, Japan

Cover: Foto ©Suzi / pixelio.de

More available books at **www.hansebooks.com**

THE

POLITICAL CRISIS OF 1861.

A REPLY TO MR. BLAINE,

BY

CHRISTOPHER STUART PATTERSON.

PHILADELPHIA:
PORTER & COATES.
1884.

Printed by
ALLEN, LANE & SCOTT,
Philadelphia.

THE published chapter of Mr. Blaine's book deals with that crisis in the history of the country which culminated in civil war. The distinguishing characteristic of Mr. Blaine's literary workmanship is in his directness of appeal to his reader's sympathies and prejudices. His point of view is that of the advocate and not that of the judge, and that portion of his book which has been given to the public is a printed oration and not an historical essay. Yet were his subject less important, and were his style less attractive, his words would command attention, because of popular appreciation of the brilliant certainties of his past, and popular interest in the still more brilliant possibilities of his future.

Mr. Blaine's conclusion is that Mr. Buchanan could, by prompt and vigorous action, have suppressed the rebellion, and changed the course of history; and he necessarily bases this conclusion upon the assumption that the lawful exercise of executive authority would have crushed the revolt in its incipiency. That assumption involves a misapprehension of the relative powers of the legislative and executive departments of the government of the United States, a misunderstanding of the actual condition of public affairs in the latter part of 1860 and early part of 1861, and an inadequate appreciation of Mr. Buchanan's clearness of perception and earnestness of purpose.

Mr. Blaine does no more than justice to the purity, he does less than justice to the strength, of Mr. Buchanan's character. Stripped of all rhetorical forms of expression, and plainly stated, his estimate of Mr. Buchanan is, that he was a conscientious but timid man, who was habitually influenced by the stronger minds of those with whom he came in contact. It is true that this estimate differs from that which was for a long time the popular impression of Mr. Buchanan's character, only in that it gives him credit for integrity of purpose; yet a careful study of the actual condition of public affairs in 1860 and 1861, and a dispassionate view of the difficulties which beset Mr. Buchanan's administration in its closing days, ought to convince any one that Mr. Buchanan is entitled to a higher measure of consideration than that which Mr. Blaine has accorded to him.

Fortunately the materials for the formation of an accurate judgment with regard to the policy and the action of Mr. Buchanan's administration are within the reach of every man, for those materials are to be found, not only in the journals of Congress, in the Presidential messages and other State papers of the day, in Mr. Buchanan's published account of his administration, and in the memoirs and letters of other active participants in the great events of that time, but also in those lately published volumes in which Mr. George Ticknor Curtis has, with historical accuracy, with adequate fullness of detail, and with a judicial impartiality, as admirable as it is rare among biographers, told the story of Mr. Buchanan's life. He who considers and weighs this mass of evidence will not fail to conclude that the Mr. Buchanan of history is a very different person from the timid old man, honest but infirm of purpose, and devoid of moral vertebræ, that Mr. Blaine's canvas presents to us.

Mr. Buchanan came of that Scotch-Irish stock, which, combining in varying proportions the perseverance, caution. and self-reliance of the Scottish, and the enthusiasm, sympathy, and unselfishness of the Irish character, has given to England many of her great soldiers and statesmen, and has furnished to the United States no inconsiderable proportion of the brain as well as of the bone and sinew of its population. Called to the bar in 1812, he had rapidly achieved distinction, and his professional success was attested by the entries in his fee book, by the character of the causes in which he was retained, and by his successful advocacy of those causes. In public life he had won, in speedy succession, the little and the great prizes of political ambition. After a term of preliminary service in the lower House of the Legislature of Pennsylvania, he had been from 1821 to 1831 a representative in Congress; from 1831 to 1833 minister to the court of St. Petersburg; from 1834 to 1845 a Senator of the United States; from 1845 to 1849 the Secretary of State in the Cabinet of President Polk; and from 1853 to 1856 minister to England. In 1856 he had been selected as the standard-bearer of his party, because he was universally recognized as the ablest representative of that party's principles, and in 1857 he became the President of the United States.

In Congress Mr. Buchanan studied the subject of discussion with the same care with which he prepared his cases at the bar. He almost always spoke at the latest possible stage of the debate, thus enabling himself to take advantage of the errors and omissions of previous speakers, and his reported speeches are well reasoned arguments from which nothing is omitted which could serve to explain and vindicate the view he advocated. Year after year he joined issue in debate with Webster, Clay, Clayton, and the many other able men who were the consistent opponents of Democratic doctrines. With them he discussed great questions upon broad grounds of constitutional authority and political expediency, and he maintained the independence of his judgment against their persuasive reasoning. In the Cabinet, and at the courts of Russia and of England, he was called to shape and to present the national policy as affecting the relations of the country to foreign states; he negotiated a commercial treaty at St. Petersburg; he stated with precision and maintained with firmness the position of the United States with regard to its north-western boundary; in the complications growing out of the misconstruction of the Clayton-Bulwer treaty, he asserted the Monroe doctrine in relation to South American affairs with a vigour that might well command the sympathy and challenge the admiration of Mr. Blaine; and by the discovery that "the simple dress of an American citizen" is the ordinary evening attire of a gentleman with the addition of a sword, he, while doubtless laughing in his sleeve, accomplished, with a more than diplomatic gravity, the pacific settlement of that momentous controversy as to the proper garb of a Republican representative accredited to a monarchical court, which Mr. Secretary Marcy had provoked as the first step in a sartorial propaganda of Democratic doctrines. No one, who fails to study the dispatches which Mr. Buchanan wrote when Secretary of State and Minister to England, can do full justice to his ability, for in moderation of tone, in clearness of statement, and in logical accuracy of reasoning, they are models of diplomatic communication.

Yet Mr. Buchanan could not claim to rival Horace Walpole or Lord Chesterfield as a letter writer. Few readers of the many and lengthy letters which Mr. Curtis prints will be likely to concur in the biographer's approval of their literary merits. Mr. Buchanan in private intercourse wrote too often, too rapidly, and too carelessly to write well. Many as are the letters which Mr. Curtis prints, they constitute but a small part of Mr. Buchanan's epistolary efforts. No more voluminous letter writer ever lived. Mr. Curtis does not state it, but it is a fact well known to those who were Mr. Buchanan's political associates and adherents, that one means by which he created and increased his influence in his party, was by the writing of private letters, not only to leaders in national, state, or municipal politics, but also to politicians of lesser note. Those letters flattered the recipients, and, passing from hand to hand, they made Mr. Buchanan's name a household word throughout the country. The man, whose ambition nerved him to devote hours of every working-day to the writing of such practical epistles, had no time to waste on the graces of style, the refinements of sentiment, or humorous turns of expression.

Mr. Buchanan had entered public life as a member of the Democratic party; to its favour he owed all the offices he held; and by its votes he was placed in the Presidency. For the greater part of seventy years that party had controlled the government of the United States. It had maintained against the centralizing tendencies of the Federal party, the reserved rights of the States, and the paramount necessity of a strict construction of the Constitution; it had opposed the appropriation of the public money to works of internal improvement; it had resisted the establishment of a national bank, the emission of a paper currency, and the imposition of any tariff which should fail to afford equal protection to every section of the Union; it had vigorously prosecuted the war of 1812 with England and the war of 1847 with Mexico; in 1832 it had suppressed rebellion in South Carolina by the prompt assertion of the supremacy of the Federal Government; it had at all times in its history consistently asserted the exemption of slavery in the

States from federal interference, and the obligation of the Northern States to surrender fugitive slaves; and in 1860, broken into discordant factions by irreconcilable differences of opinion upon the question of slavery in the Territories, it was driven from power, and Mr. Buchanan, charged with the administration of the government, and supported only by a disorganized and defeated party, was confronted by a rebellion, whose leaders had been his political allies and his personal friends.

That rebellion was not a sudden outburst of popular fury, but it was the inevitable result of causes that were slow of growth, yet certain of operation. At the close of the war of the Revolution, the thirteen colonies which had successfully asserted their independence, did not constitute a homogeneous nation. The nearest settlements of those scantily populated States were then separated from each other by distances, whose effect in retarding or preventing communication can with difficulty be realized in these days of railways, telegraphs, newspapers, and hourly mails. But, widely separated as they were in distance and in time, they were still more widely separated by differences in the sources and manner of their original settlement, and in the character of their institutions, and of all those differences the most important were those that found their last expression in the essential antagonism of slavery to free institutions.

Slaves had been imported into the colonies under

British rule, and, at the end of the war of Independence, Delaware, Maryland, Virginia, the two Carolinas, and Georgia had a slave population of more than half a million, while Pennsylvania, New Jersey, New York, Connecticut, Massachusetts, Vermont, and Rhode Island were slave States only in name. Their climate, then temperate in summer and very cold in winter, permitted the employment of white men in the fields, and slave labour being brought into competition with free labour was, as it always will be, discovered to be less economical. Under the teaching of self-interest, those States were soon permeated by a realizing sense of the evils of slavery, which found practical expression in the more or less gradual emancipation of all the slaves within the limits of their jurisdiction. While an intelligent appreciation of the necessary evils of slavery was then so far from being peculiar to the Northern States that many Southern statesmen were outspoken abolitionists, yet so large a relative proportion of the wealth of the South was invested in slave property, and slave labour was so generally regarded in the South as essential to the cultivation of rice, indigo, and tobacco, that, even under the confederation, the States had ranged themselves under the opposing banners of freedom and slavery. The confederation in which the colonies had united on the successful issue of the war of independence was soon found to be a rope of sand, and, in the words of the preamble to the Constitution of the United States, it became necessary "in order to form a more perfect union, establish justice, insure domestic tranquillity, provide for the common defence, promote the general welfare, and secure the blessings of liberty," that for the confederation of States, there should be substituted an union of the people of the United States under a federal government, which though limited in its action by the reservation to the several States of all powers not in express terms delegated to the United States, should yet be supreme within its defined bounds.

The union under one federal government of States whose laws sanctioned, with States whose laws forbade, slavery rendered it essential to the conservation of slavery, that its status should be recognized by the federal constitution as that of a domestic institution of the States exempted from federal interference, that the extradition of fugitive slaves should be imposed as a duty binding upon the free States, and that the balance of power, as between the free and the slave States, should be so constituted and so maintained that no subsequent alteration of the terms of union should impair the security of slavery. The Constitution was formed upon these principles. The North and the South each gained all the advantages that were to be derived from the union, but the South gained also the recognition of slavery as a subject of State and not of national regulation; the admission of the right to reclaim fugitive slaves; the postponement until 1808 of the prohibition of the slave trade; the limitation to ten dollars *per capita* of the

customs duty upon imported slaves; the concession
that in the computation of the population for the purpose of representation in the popular branch of the
national legislature, three-fifths of the whole number
of slaves in each State should be added to the number of free men of that State; and the equality of
representation of the States in the Senate of the
United States. The effect of these constitutional
guaranties was not only to protect slavery from
federal interference under the Constitution as then
framed, but also to forbid any amendment of that
Constitution in the interest of abolition, so long as
the slave States constituted more than one-fourth
of the whole number of States. Thenceforward
slavery in the States was legally unassailable by
either the Federal Government or the free States.

Yet, here and there, throughout the North, there
came together earnest men and women, who saw so
vividly the inherent wrong of slavery, that they
hungered and thirsted for its destruction; and, alike
unmindful of the protection which the Constitution
had thrown around the thing they hated, of their
duty as citizens to respect that legal immunity, and
of the practical effect of their action in uniting the
people of the Southern States in the defence of
slavery, they began and continued, by written and
by spoken words, an aggressive political campaign for
its abolition. It is true that that agitation destroyed
that which, in 1832, seemed to be the fair promise of
voluntary abolition in Virginia, and it is also true

that the same cause, at a later day, postponed abolition in the District of Columbia; but it is equally
true that every attempt by a Southern man to reclaim
his fugitive slave and forcibly carry him back from
freedom into slavery; every effort by the South
to aggrandize slavery by the admission of new slave
States; and every endeavour, upon the part of Northern conservatives. to suppress the abolitionists by
social and political proscription, only added fresh
fuel to the flames of agitation.

As we read the history of the United States,
from 1787 to 1860, as war has since recorded it in
letters of fire and blood, we can see clearly that
there never was a day in all those years when it
would not have been, in those who then led public
opinion, the highest duty of statesmanship to secure,
at whatever cost in money, the voluntary abolition
of slavery, and thus to have ended in peace the
irreconcilable conflict of opinion between those who
could see only the barbarity, the cruelty, and the
individual and national demoralization of slavery, and
those others who could see only its constitutional
recognition and legal immunity. In 1828 one Northern man at least, who had no sympathy with slavery,
saw clearly that which was at one and the same time
the path of duty and of national self-interest. Dr.
William Ellery Channing,* in that year wrote to

---

* The letter is referred to by Mr. Curtis in the second volume of his life
of Mr. Buchanan, page 296, and is printed in full in Mr. Webster's works,
vol. V., page 367.

Mr. Webster, "It seems to me that, before moving in this matter, we ought to say to them" (the Southern States) "distinctly, 'we consider slavery as your calamity, not your crime, and we will share with you the burden of putting an end to it. We will consent that the public lands shall be appropriated to this object; or that the general government shall be clothed with power to apply a portion of revenue to it.'   *   *   *   We must first let the Southern States see that we are their *friends* in this affair; that we sympathize with them, and, from principles of patriotism and philanthropy, are willing to share the toil and expense of abolishing slavery, or I fear our interference will avail nothing."   *   *   *   *   *   *
"My fear in regard to our efforts against slavery is, that we shall make the case worse by rousing sectional pride and passion for its support, and that we shall only break the country into two great parties, which may shake the foundations of government."

But Dr. Channing's wise counsels did not prevail, for not until the light of battle shone in men's faces did the country realize that slavery had been at all times a standing menace to its peace; nor, in the days of restricted national expenditure which preceded the war, could any party, even if the public conscience had been awakened, and if the South had voluntarily accepted emancipation, have gone to the country with any hope of success upon the issue of a national appropriation for the liberation of slaves.

Therefore it was that efforts were made, from time
to time, by successive compromises, to remove the
slavery question from the range of political discussion, but each compromise in its turn, though at the
time accepted as a finality, failed of accomplishing
its desired end, because of its inability to destroy
the irritating cause, and because of its essential in-
applicability to changed circumstances and conditions. In truth. the conflict between freedom and
slavery was, as Mr. Seward said, irrepressible. On
the one side was the North, with its diversified in-
terests and industries, and with its conscience slowly
but surely awakening to a realizing sense of the
evils of slavery, and, as the necessary result of free
institutions, rapidly increasing in population and in
wealth ; and on the other side was the agricultural
South, united as one man in resistance to what it
regarded as a threatened invasion of its rights of
property, and a menace of the horrors of a servile
insurrection, repelling free immigration, and striving
to build up additional bulwarks for slavery in the
creation of new slave States.

The Constitution having, as the price of union,
exempted slavery in the States from federal interference, the Territories became the theatre of the
struggle for the balance of power. An ordinance
of the confederation, confirmed in express terms by
the First Congress, and recognized by the admission
of Ohio, Indiana, and Illinois as free States, had
dedicated to freedom the territory north-west of the

Ohio river. The compromise of 1820 admitted Missouri as a slave State, and designated the parallel of 36° 30′ as the dividing line between freedom and slavery in the remainder of the territory acquired from France by the treaty of 1803. The compromise of 1850 gave to the South a new fugitive slave law, intended to be more efficacious than the then existing law of 1793, and the organization of territorial governments in New Mexico and Utah, with the guarantee of the admission of those Territories as States "with or without slavery, as their respective constitutions might require," and secured to the North the prohibition of the domestic slave trade in the District of Columbia and the immediate admission of California as a free State. It was then hoped that the slavery question had ceased to be a practical issue in national politics, but this hope was not possible of fulfillment, for the census of 1850 told the South that constitutional compact and legislative compromise alike had failed to resist the aggressive force of free institutions, and that, in the struggle for the balance of power, the North had won. When the Constitution was formed, the free States and the slave States had been nearly equal in population and in political power, but before 1860 it had come to pass that there were eighteen free States with thirty-six votes in the Senate, one hundred and forty-seven votes in the House, and one hundred and eighty-three electoral votes, while there were but fifteen slave States, with thirty votes in the Senate, ninety votes in the House, and one hundred and twenty electoral votes. Yet no amendment to the federal constitution could even then have been adopted in opposition to which the slave States had been united, for their relative strength was sufficient, not only to forbid the ratification of any such amendment, but also to prevent its preliminary approval by the Congress, and to prohibit the calling of a convention to consider any amendment whatever. Nor was the numerical inferiority of the South in representation in the Congress and in the electoral college of much practical importance so long as the united South should not be opposed by a united North.

But in 1854 the dragon's teeth were sown broadcast, that later were to spring up armed men, for, in that year, with the ostensible purpose of vindicating the inherent sovereignty of the people, whether exercised by territorial or by State legislatures, but with a real and practical intent to regain, by the admission of new slave States, the lost supremacy of the South, the Missouri Compromise was repealed, and the Territories were thrown open to the invading march of slavery. But the doctrine of territorial autonomy, though originated by Northern Democrats, did not go far enough to satisfy the South, and it was promptly antagonized within the Democratic party by the assertion of the indefeasible right of the slave owner to hold slaves, as property, in all the Territories of the United States. As has so often been the case, extravagant demands upon the one side were met by equally extravagant demands upon the other, and the Republican party signalized its entrance upon the stage of national politics by the declaration that all the Territories of the United States were irrevocably dedicated to freedom.[*] Neither of the conflicting doctrines could find adequate support in the Constitution, which, by its guarded recognition of slavery, defined it as the creature of State law and thereby localized its operation, and which had, in express terms, empowered Congress to legislate for the Territories, nor in that governmental practice which had admitted Territories as free or slave States, according to the terms of their respective constitutions when accepted by Congress. Such were the issues raised for popular decision in the presidential contest of 1860, which resulted, for the first time in our history, in the choice of a President who owed his election to Northern votes only.

That memorable canvass found the country in an excited state of feeling which prohibited dispassionate consideration or calm discussion. Several causes had contributed to this result.

Two days after the inauguration of Mr. Buchanan, the Supreme Court of the United States had attempted, for the second time in its history, to determine by a judicial deliverance a question upon

---

[*] If the Republican party had limited its declaration upon this subject to the assertion of the expediency of admitting no more slave States, it would have avoided just criticism, but its statement that the normal condition of all the Territories was that of freedom was neither historically accurate, nor well founded in constitutional law.

which political parties were at issue. In 1803, in
the case of Marbury *vs.* Madison,* judges, who were
Federalists, had endeavored to deprive the Democratic party of those spoils of office which it regarded as the fruits of its triumph over the Federal party. In 1857, in the Dred Scott case,†
judges, who were Democrats, sought to establish the
indefeasible right of slavery to occupy the Territories of the United States. The cases were alike,
in that, in each instance, the court proved, to its
own satisfaction, that it had no jurisdiction over the
subject-matter of its decision, and that, in each instance, the country revolted against the attempted
judicial usurpation of political functions. In the
Dred Scott case the record raised severally the
questions of the citizenship of a free negro, and of
the effect upon the status of a negro held to slavery
under the laws of Missouri, of a removal to, and
residence with, his master in the free State of Illinois and in the territory of Wisconsin north of the
Missouri Compromise line. As the jurisdiction of
the court was dependent upon the citizenship of the
parties, it was not only incumbent upon the plaintiff to maintain his averment of citizenship, but it
was obligatory upon the court to find in his favour
as to that, before it could express any other than
an extra-judicial opinion upon the merits of the
cause. In an hour, that was evil alike for the dig-

* Reported in 1 Cranch, 137.
† Reported in 19 Howard, 393.

nity and for the judicial reputation of the court and
for the peace of the country, a majority of the
judges of that high tribunal succeeded in convinc-
ing themselves that they could, with judicial propri-
ety and logical consistency, so determine the merits
of a cause, of which they refused to take jurisdiction, as not only to conclude the parties to the liti-
gation, but also to bind the conscience of the country. The voluminous opinions of the judges who
constituted the majority of the court, do more credit
to their learning and to their industry than to their
reasoning powers, and every argument which they
put forward was more than answered in the master-
ly dissenting opinion of Mr. Justice Curtis. They
denied the citizenship of free negroes, although it is
an historical fact that, in five of the thirteen original States, negroes were not only recognized as citizens but also admitted to the exercise of the right
of suffrage, and, although many acts of Congress
had by necessary implication recognized negroes as
citizens. They declared the Missouri Compromise
unconstitutional, upon the narrow ground that that
clause in the Constitution which delegated to Congress the "power to dispose of and make all need-
ful rules and regulations respecting the territory or
other property belonging to the United States,"
could operate only upon such territory as the
United States had when the Constitution was
adopted, and that Congress could exercise over sub-
sequently acquired territory no power which should

impair the right of slave owners to take their slaves into that territory and hold them there, and, in so deciding, they not only ignored the accepted construction of the Constitution, as settled by more than sixty years of unquestioned legislation, but they also gave to the purely municipal institution of slavery an extra-territorial force which was as foreign to public law as it was unwarranted by the most liberal construction of the Constitution. They disposed of the effect claimed by the plaintiff for his residence on free soil, by treating it as a question, not of Illinois or of Wisconsin law, but of the effect which Missouri should give to that law, and they found the law of Missouri on that subject, in a late decision of the Supreme Court of Missouri, which was at variance with many prior decisions of the same court. forgetting that they had but lately decided * that, while the courts of the United States do in general feel themselves bound to receive and adopt. without examination or further inquiry, that settled construction of the law of a State which has been established by its highest judicature, yet, where the decisions of a State court are not consistent, the courts of the United States do not feel bound to follow the last.

The announcement of the judgment of the court failed of its intended pacificatory effect; it impaired popular confidence in the independence and impartiality of the court; it destroyed all that remained

* Pease vs. Peck, 18 Howard, 595.

of faith in the sanctity of political compromises; and it added to the growing distrust of the peaceful solution of the slavery problem.

The repeal of the Missouri Compromise having renewed the anti-slavery agitation in its most dangerous form, by inviting a struggle in each Territory for the control of the territorial government in the interest of freedom or of slavery, that struggle was, in Kansas, not confined to the ordinary methods of political discussion, but was marked by riots and bloodshed, and the pro-slavery party obtained, by fraud and force, a complete control of the territorial organization, and thereby secured, under President Pierce's administration, such a recognition by the legislative department of the Federal Government as necessarily deprived Mr. Buchanan, when President, of all executive discretion in the matter.

Those disgraceful disturbances, which have given to "bleeding Kansas" its unhappy fame, outraged the North; in 1859 the John Brown raid drove the South to the verge of madness; and in 1860 the disruption of the Democratic party, hopelessly divided by jealousies between its leaders and dissensions among their followers, and no less by irreconcilable differences of opinion as to the extension of slavery in the Territories, gave to the Republican party its first national victory. In the then temper of the public mind the popular verdict, though recorded with all the forms of law, could not be expected to receive the cheerful acquiescence of the defeated

party; yet there could be no possible question as
to the regularity of Mr. Lincoln's election, nor as
to the validity of his title to the Presidency, nor
was there in the triumph of the Republican party,
apart from its abstract assertion of the essentially free
character of all the Territories, any menace of revolutionary action as against the South. Its platform
had in express terms admitted the right of the
States to regulate, without federal interference, their
domestic affairs; and, while it is true that the fet-
ters of political platforms sit lightly upon party
consciences, yet the South was not forced to rely
upon the moderation of the victorious party, but
was adequately protected against hostile action
within the limits of the Constitution by the conservatism of the great mass of people, and also
against aggression beyond those limits by the conceded power of the Supreme Court to annul unconstitutional legislation. Never, therefore, was there
greater madness than that of those misguided leaders of public opinion who raised the standard of rebellion. No man among them, in his inmost heart,
believed or hoped that the South would, by conquest,
reduce the States of the North to the condition of
subject provinces. The most that they expected or
desired was, that the Southern States would suc-
ceed in freeing themselves from the federal yoke. If
they had so succeeded, no standing army would have
been large enough to so thoroughly patrol the frontier
separating them from the free States of the North

as to effectually prevent the escape of slaves, and no treaty between the South and the North stipulating for the rendition of the fugitives would, if such a treaty could have been negotiated and enforced, have been half as efficacious as even the fugitive slave law had been. The South, by successful rebellion, could not possibly gain for slavery any greater immunity than that which the Constitution and the laws of the United States threw around it, and they would, with equal certainty, have lost by the termination of the federal compact that privilege of free trade between the North and South which, in economic value to them, far exceeded the conservation of slavery.

There was much in the past history of the country that tended to mislead the South. In each of the successive crises of the slavery question Southern threats of disunion had been met by Northern concessions, and upon each occasion the South had gained by compromise all that it demanded. The formation of the Constitution, the struggle in 1820 over the admission of Missouri, the nullification controversy terminated by Mr. Clay's compromise tariff, the annexation of Texas, the war with Mexico, and the recent settlement of 1850, ratified by the triumphant election of President Pierce, might well convince superficial observers that Southern firmness would be encountered only by Northern weakness, but those who reasoned thus did not take into their consideration the fact that, for the first time in its history, the South was confronted by a distinctively Northern party, with a defined policy, and emboldened by a national victory.

It would have been, upon the part of the Southern leaders, political wisdom to have recognized the fact that free immigration would effectually prevent the colonization and control of the Territories in the interest of slavery, and to have concentrated their efforts upon the maintenance within the Union of those constitutional guaranties, which more than adequately protected slavery in the States from federal interference. Had they done so, it is possible that the slavery question might have found its ultimate solution in a system of gradual and compensated emancipation, which, without revolution, or even social disturbance, would have made all the States free. Seventy years of strife had proven that no fugitive slave law ever could be practically enforceable in a free State, and if war had been averted there must, at no distant period, have been substituted for the rendition of fugitives from slavery the payment of a pecuniary compensation to their owners, and North and South, alike familiarized with the idea of compensation, and constantly irritated by its compulsory application to individual cases, would, ere long, have seen it to be to the common interest of the whole country to buy the freedom of all the slaves, and thus to terminate in peace that which ever had been, and ever would be, a cause of national discord. But a peaceful solution of the problem

was not possible of accomplishment, and it was
fated that the sin and wrong of slavery should find
their atonement only in blood; for, in the South, madness ruled the hour. The election of Mr. Lincoln
was promptly followed by South Carolina's threat
of secession, and the country, though it knew it not,
was brought face to face with war. Neither North
nor South had learned in their years of union to
know each other, and, least of all, to realize that,
under similar forms of government, the Southern
States were, as they had been from the first, aris-
tocracies, whose customs, more powerful than their
laws, tended to the concentration of wealth and political power in the hands of their leaders, while the
Northern States had, by the growth of population,
the development of trade and manufactures, and the
more equal distribution of wealth, become democra-
cies, in which he who would lead the people must
first discover and formulate that which the people
really desired. Therefore it was, that the North un-
derestimated the rashness of the Southern leaders,
and the power of those leaders to accomplish that
which they threatened; while the South grievously
miscalculated the loyal devotion of the people of the
North to their government, and the strength of their
determination to maintain the Union.

No man who looks back to that gulf of blood
which separates 1866 from 1860, into which North
and South alike, with reckless prodigality, threw
down their treasure and the fairest of their youth,

can doubt that it was Mr. Buchanan's first and highest duty, as President of the United States, to exercise all the influence of his high office in order to secure, if it were possible, a peaceable adjustment of those differences, which, unadjusted, threatened civil war. That duty he fully and faithfully performed. He urged upon Congress the paramount necessity of averting hostilities by reasonable measures of conciliation, and he pressed upon its consideration certain constitutional amendments, but no pacific settlement was possible. On the one side, the repeal of the Missouri Compromise and the deliverance of the judges of the Supreme Court in the Dred Scott case had destroyed popular faith in the stability of all compromises, however solemnly ratified, and however long acquiesced in ; the rash and revolutionary action of the Southern leaders had prejudiced the North against any terms of concession to rebels in arms ; and, last, but not least, not until the shot had been fired at Sumter did the North believe in the reality of war. On the other hand, the leaders of rebellion were confident that secession would be accomplished without serious opposition, and that the independence of the Southern States would be speedily recognized. For these reasons no plan of adjustment was possible of adoption, but that all such plans failed was certainly not the fault of Mr. Buchanan.

The suppression of the rebellion has been followed by political and social changes, which are too great to be measured by constitutional amendments and

statutes, and, of all those changes, the greatest is
that revolution in opinion which, working silently
in the hearts of men and never formulated into
law, has converted a confederation of States into
a nation, whose Congress and whose President now
exercise powers, and whose Supreme Court now an-
nounces doctrines which Alexander Hamilton would
have heartily approved. Verily, the whirligig of time
has more than avenged the Federalists. Their theory
of government, long despised of men, is now the accepted construction; and eighty years after their
final expulsion from power, their doctrines have
dominated the nation. But it was not so in 1861, nor
had it been so at any time since Mr. Jefferson succeeded
Mr. Adams in the Presidency. Mr. Buchanan's administration is, therefore, to be judged not as Mr. Blaine
judges it, by the standard of to-day, but by that jealous
apportionment of power between the different departments of the government which had been before 1861
prescribed by law and recognized in practice.

An absolute government, when confronted by rebellion, is limited in its action only by considerations of
expediency, and by the sufficiency of its armed force
for the suppression of that rebellion, but a constitutional, and especially a republican, government is
also hampered by those organic restraints which in-
terpose legal barriers to the exercise by the executive of the whole power of the government. Pre-
eminently was this true of the United States in
1861, for its Constitution, framed to protect the lib-

erty of the citizen, and to prevent the exercise of arbitrary power by the government, had prescribed as the President's only legal function that of enforcing, by the use of the means entrusted to him, obedience to the Constitution and the laws of Congress. It is clear, beyond the possibility of doubt, that Mr. Buchanan, however extensive might have been his lawful executive powers, and however adequate the means at his command, would not have been justified, before the Presidential election of 1860, in taking any steps which could have been construed as the expression of an opinion upon the part of the executive, that the election of the Republican candidate would certainly, or even probably, be followed by rebellion in the South. Any such action would have been rightly regarded by the country as an endeavour upon the part of the administration to deter citizens from voting the Republican ticket, by rousing in their breasts the fear that the election of that ticket would necessarily be followed by civil war. It is equally clear also that, as no overt act was committed until more than a fortnight after Congress had convened in annual session, Mr. Buchanan would not have been justified in usurping powers which had not been vested in the executive. Neither the Constitution, nor any then subsisting legislation, had conferred upon the President any authority to employ the regular army or navy, save in the defense of the Federal property, or to call out the militia for the suppression of insurrection in any State, under circumstances such as then confronted him. The Constitution had, indeed, in express terms, authorized Congress " to provide for calling forth the militia to execute the laws of the Union, suppress insurrections, and repel invasions," but Congress, in its delegation of that constitutional authority, had been so jealous of executive usurpation of the power of the sword, that it had, by statutes of 1795 and 1807, empowered the President to employ the army and navy in the suppression of insurrection within any State only " on application of the legislature of such State, or of the executive, when the legislature cannot be convened," or, in default of any such application, only in aid of the civil process of the Federal courts.* It is obvious that this limited grant vested in the President no power that could be legally used when, as in the then existing emergency, the executive and legislative authorities of South Carolina led the rebellion, and the resignation of the Federal judges and marshals had effectually prevented the issuing of any Federal process.

Charleston harbour was, until after Mr. Buchanan's retirement, the only threatened point. Major Anderson, who commanded Fort Sumter, had, with reiterated expressions of confidence, asserted the sufficiency of the force under his command for the suc-

---

* The legislation of 1833, which had been passed to enable President Jackson to meet the nullification issue, vested certain powers in the President, but only for a limited time, and that time had long since expired.

cessful defense of his post; and, not until the morning of Mr. Lincoln's inauguration, did Mr. Buchanan receive from Major Anderson any qualification of that assertion. The regular army of the United States numbered sixteen thousand officers and men, of whom only five companies, in all four hundred men, were available to reinforce the garrison in Fort Sumter, or to occupy the other forts and arsenals in the Southern States, the presence of the rest of the army being imperatively required on the Western frontier and the plains to hold the Indian tribes in check. Nor did the country possess any sufficient naval force.

Mr. Buchanan might well suppose that the inadequacy of the available military and naval forces of the government, and his legal inability to use them, or to levy additional forces, would not be of serious importance, in view of the fact that the Congress, who alone could authorize him to call out the militia, and who alone could appropriate the necessary money, would convene in annual session more than a fortnight before South Carolina could put into action its threat of rebellion, and would remain in session during the remainder of his administration. He, therefore, in his annual message of 3d December, 1860, and in his special message of 8th January, 1861, fully disclosed to Congress the nature of the emergency, and explained his inability to cope with it unless larger powers were conferred upon him, but those powers Congress failed to grant. That significant want of action by Congress was not due to any careless oversight, nor to any Democratic sympathy with rebellion, but it was the deliberate expression of that defined policy of the leaders of the Republican party which advisedly reserved, for the incoming administration, the adjustment of the pending national difficulties, and which carefully avoided any legislation, either in the direction of conciliation or coercion, that might have a tendency to affect Mr. Lincoln's independence of action.

That policy was, so far as it sought to postpone the consideration of terms of compromise until after Mr. Lincoln's inauguration, not only recommended by motives of party expediency, but also supported by higher considerations. For the country to buy, by concession, the peaceful inauguration of a President who had been duly elected, was a dangerous precedent. The election of Mr. Lincoln had shown that the Democrats were in a minority in the North, and that that minority was far from unanimous. The Republicans, therefore, naturally insisted, not only that Mr. Lincoln should be peaceably inaugurated, but also that the negotiations should be conducted upon the part of the North by that party to whom the North had so decisively entrusted the responsibility of administration. But it may well be questioned whether it would not have been better to have armed Mr. Buchanan with the power of the sword, and thus to have impressed the South with the strength of Northern determination. But, however that may be. it does not become the Republican party to avoid its just responsibility for its Congres-sional inaction in 1861, and to seek to hold Mr. Buchanan responsible for not doing that which it refused to clothe him with power to effect. Unprovided with adequate means of coercion, and not permitted to under-take the accomplishment of a final and pacific adjust-ment of the national difficulties, it was clearly Mr. Bu-chanan's only duty to so administer the government during the brief remaining portion of his term that rebel-lion should be induced to stay its hand, that other Southern States should be, if possible, prevented from joining forces with South Carolina, and that Mr. Lin-coln should, in his administration of the government, be unhampered by any act or omission of his predecessor.

Mr. Chase, afterwards the Secretary of the Treas-ury in Mr. Lincoln's Cabinet, put this view forcibly in a letter,* which he wrote to Mr. Seward, on 11th January, 1861, in which he said :—

"You are to be Secretary of State.   *   *   * Let me urge you to give countenance to no scheme of compromise. Mr. Lincoln will be inaugurated in a few days. Then the Republicans will be charged with the responsibility of administration. Then, too, they will control one branch of the Government. To me it seems all important that no compromise be now made, and no concession involving any surren-der of principles; but that the people of the slave

---

* Life and Public Services of Salmon Portland Chase, by J. W. Schuckers, page 202.

States, and of all the States, be plainly told that the Republicans have no proposition to make at present; that when they have the power they will be ready to offer an adjustment fair and beneficial to all sections of the country—that, in the meantime, all they ask of those who now have the power is, to uphold the Constitution, maintain the Union, and enforce the laws."

This duty Mr. Buchanan took upon himself, and he performed it with unfaltering courage and unswerving fidelity. Read in the light of this purpose, his words and his acts were as wise as they were consistent. His last annual message was addressed to Congress, but intended as an appeal to his countrymen, both North and South. In it he conceded the existence of that right of revolution, which is the last recourse of a people oppressed by intolerable tyranny, and by whose exercise, in 1776, the independence of the United States was achieved, but he proved to the South that existing circumstances did not justify revolution; * he demonstrated the logical fallacy and the practical folly of secession; with a clear appreciation of the complex character of the Federal Government, which, while recognizing the autonomy of the States, yet compels the citizens of those States to obey the laws of the

* Mr. Blaine, in criticising Mr. Buchanan's reference to the right of revolution, did not remember that Mr. Lincoln said, in his inaugural address, "This country, with its institutions, belongs to the people who inhabit it. Whenever they shall grow weary of the existing government, they can exercise their constitutional right of amending it, or their revolutionary right to dismember or overthrow it."

United States, he admitted the legal inability of the
Federal Government to coerce the political action of,
or to make war upon a State, but he as clearly asserted the right of the United States to defend its
property and to maintain the supremacy of its laws,
and the accuracy of this distinction was conceded
by the official acts and declarations of the succeed-
ing administration; he recommended that which he
regarded as an equitable adjustment of the pending
difficulties; he threw upon Congress the responsibility of legislation; and he exhorted the madmen of
the hour to pause before they destroyed the Union.
In his special message he again asked for power to
act, and he again urged upon Congress the duty of
adjustment. In his actions he made no concessions
to rebels, he maintained the forces of the Union in
Charleston and Pensacola harbours, he filled the va-
cancies in his Cabinet by the appointment of officers
whose loyalty was unquestionable, he sacrificed to his
public duty his party affiliations and his personal
friendships, and, on the 4th of March, 1861, he relin-
quished the Presidency, having taken every wise pre-
caution for the peaceable inauguration of Mr. Lincoln.

Mr. Lincoln said in his inaugural address: " The
power confided to me will be used to hold, occupy,
and possess the property and places belonging to the
Government, and to collect the duties and imposts;
but, beyond what may be but necessary for these
objects, there will be no invasion, no using of force
against or among the people anywhere. Where hos-

tility to the United States in any interior locality shall be so great and universal as to prevent competent resident citizens from holding the Federal offices, there will be no attempt to force obnoxious strangers among the people for that object. While the strict legal right may exist in the Government to enforce the exercise of these offices, the attempt to do so would be so irritating, and so nearly impracticable withal, I deem it better to forego, for the time, the uses of such offices.

"The mails, unless repelled, will continue to be furnished in all parts of the Union. So far as possible, the people everywhere shall have that sense of perfect security which is most favourable to calm thought and reflection. The course here indicated will be followed, unless current events and experience shall show a modification or change to be proper, and in every case and exigency my best discretion will be exercised according to circumstances actually existing, and with a view and a hope of a peaceful solution of the national troubles, and the restoration of fraternal sympathies and affections." Mr. Seward, then the Secretary of State in Mr. Lincoln's Cabinet, said in a dispatch * addressed to Mr. Adams, then in London, and dated but two days before the bombardment of Sumter, " the President on the one hand will not suffer the Federal authority to fall into abeyance, nor will he on the other hand aggravate existing evils by attempts at coercion which must assume the form of direct war against any of the revolutionary States."

* Quoted by Mr. Curtis, Vol. II. page 351.

By these official declarations Mr. Lincoln and Mr. Seward announced as the policy of the Republican administration a course of action which cannot be distinguished from that which Mr. Buchanan had laid down for himself and to which he had consistently adhered. There can, therefore, be no condemnation of Mr. Buchanan for lack of determination, or want of action, in his dealing with rebellion, which does not equally censure Mr. Lincoln and his Republican administration.

Mr. Buchanan brought to the discharge of the duties of the Presidency, maturity of judgment, a long and intimate acquaintance with the practical workings of the Federal Government, a wide and varied knowledge of men and of affairs, and an earnest determination to do his duty. It was but natural that his age, his conservatism of temperament, and his political training, should induce him to condemn both Northern and Southern extremists, and to find, in the strict enforcement of constitutional obligations, an adequate remedy for all existing evils. That which Mr. Blaine has characterized as Mr. Buchanan's timidity, was only the caution which was the necessary effect of his intelligent appreciation of the gravity of the crisis, his conscientious sense of official responsibility, and his accurate perception of the legal limitations upon his executive action. Nor do the facts sustain the distinction which Mr. Blaine seeks to draw between the Mr. Buchanan of December, 1860, and the Mr. Buchanan of January, 1861, and which attributes to the influence of Judge Black a radical change in the policy of the administration. It was not likely that, after forty years of conspicuous public service, Mr. Buchanan would have permitted his judgment to be controlled or his action to be dictated by his cabinet officers, who were, Judge Black not excepted, as inferior to him in intellectual attainments as they were lacking in official experience. This conclusion, in itself so inherently probable, is more than confirmed by the facts, which prove that Mr. Buchanan was in all respects and at all times the responsible chief of his own administration, and that its policy was shaped in accordance with his, and not others', convictions of his public duty. Nor in reality was there any change in the policy of Mr. Buchanan's administration after December, 1860. Mr. Buchanan's last annual message was framed after full consultation with his attorney-general, and those portions of the message to which Mr. Blaine most strongly takes exception only express in another form the views which Judge Black had stated a few days before in an official opinion, which Mr. Curtis prints in full.

Mr. Blaine's criticism is only destructive. He neither does, nor can, suggest any course of action upon Mr. Buchanan's part, which would, in fact, have averted war. The appeal to arms was the culmination of an embittered sectional controversy of more than seventy years' duration, and the inevitable result of the effort to unite opposing political forces under one government. Mr. Buchanan was armed neither with the power of the purse, nor with that of the sword. Under such conditions, threatenings of authority and persuasions to peace were alike useless, and attempts at coercion would have been both irritating and ineffective.

In the United States an ex-President is relegated to a position of insignificance. His political career and his party influence are ended. He can no longer reward his friends nor punish his enemies. His personal and official triumphs are alike forgotten. Those whom he appointed to office do not remember him, for with most men gratitude for favours granted is an emotion of a transient and feeble character, while in every village there are those who never forget that he slighted their fancied claims to political preferment. Mr. Buchanan not only suffered the slights and endured the contumely to which all ex-Presidents of the United States are subjected, but he was also the victim of calumny and injustice to a greater extent, by reason of the peculiar circumstances of his retirement. The Democratic party of the Northern States, shorn of the prestige of office, dispirited by the victory of its opponents at the polls, discredited by the participation of its Southern allies with rebellion, and hopelessly divided by dissensions between those of its members who, in the hour of the nation's peril, subordinated their party fealty to their civic duty, and those other of its members who ranked party above country, was in no condition to render effectual support to any man. On the other hand, the Republican party, then represented in the executive and legislative departments of the Government by comparatively new and untried men, and called with an empty treasury, with shattered national credit, and without a standing army to confront the South in armed rebellion, was ready to hold the retiring administration responsible for all the difficulties with which its successors were compelled to grapple. It is not surprising, under these circumstances, that during the clash of arms, and even after the war had ended, but while the passions which the conflict had excited were yet raging, that that which might fairly be urged in Mr. Buchanan's defence, should have failed to receive due consideration; but now, when nearly twenty years have passed away, since the irresistible logic of Appomattox closed the debate which had been opened at Sumter, it ought to be possible for the American people to discard political prejudice, and in the calm exercise of a passionless judgment, to do that justice to the memory of one of their dead Presidents which they denied to him while living.

The truth of history is of greater importance than the glorification of any political party. The fair fame of a statesman is the common inheritance of his countrymen. It is, therefore, to the best interest of all, North and South, Republicans and Democrats alike, that the sober second thought of the country should not stamp with its judgment of approval Mr. Blaine's mistaken view of the crisis of 1861.